BALANCE IN
Action

Adopting a Life Philosophy
That Works!

MELISSA GRAY

WESTBOW
PRESS®
A DIVISION OF THOMAS NELSON
& ZONDERVAN

WestBow Press books may be ordered through booksellers or by contacting:

WestBow Press
A Division of Thomas Nelson & Zondervan
1663 Liberty Drive
Bloomington, IN 47403
www.westbowpress.com
1 (866) 928-1240

Scripture quotations taken from the New English Bible,
copyright © Cambridge University Press and Oxford
University Press 1961, 1970. All rights reserved.

ISBN: 978-1-9736-3338-9 (sc)
ISBN: 978-1-9736-3339-6 (e)

Library of Congress Control Number: 2018907951

Print information available on the last page.

WestBow Press rev. date: 08/09/2018

I dedicate this book to my family.
I love you with all my heart.

Introduction

This book was inspired by the hundreds of people I have had the privilege to pray with, mentor, and walk alongside on their journey toward wholeness and healing. When my husband and I were youth pastors, it was a joy to watch the young people grow up into amazing adults. When we started serving at our church, we noticed that many of the adults never had the opportunity to be poured into in the same way these young people had. My hope is that this book will be a toolbox full of guidelines for living a balanced life, mind, body, and soul, so all of us can enjoy to the fullest—the life for which we were created.

I have often wondered throughout the years why life can seem so out of control. Why do so many of us struggle in marriages, in raising children, with addictions, sickness, or with just a vague sense that there must be something more? Shouldn't it be different? Shouldn't life be rich and full? The answer is most assuredly yes! But sadly, all too often life doesn't feel this way. Well, I for one am not willing to accept this. Our lives should be balanced. We should be filled with peace despite our circumstances. We should be healthy and strong, have sound minds, and be able to face whatever gets thrown at us with courage and endurance. The question is how? How do we experience peace when life circumstances knock us off course? We were created mind, body, and soul, three parts intended to function as a whole in perfect harmony. Yet at times these parts can become out of sync. We can over or under emphasize one area of the whole, and our lives can become suddenly dissonant. Like the three-legged stool, each leg must function at its full strength and with equal emphasis or the stool can easily topple. Each chapter of this book will contain some thoughts on the mind, body, and soul. As we focus on all three of these areas, my hope is to journey together into a life of balance, freedom, and joy.

Chapter 1: Pay attention
- Pay attention.
- Think about what you are eating and why.
- Ask Jesus to shine His light into your soul and reveal anything of importance

Chapter 2: Lies
- What lie am I believing about myself or God?
- Does it really matter what I eat?
- The ultimate lie of the soul is shame that says I need to hide and have secrets.

Chapter 3: Drinking Poison
- If we don't forgive, it's like drinking poison and expecting the other person to die.
- Forgiveness does not mean saying what was done to us is okay.

- Unforgiveness can cause sickness.
- We must forgive ourselves because we have been made completely clean by the cross.

Chapter 4: Anxiety and Depression
- We can choose to focus on the fear or focus on the good.
- Sugar feeds anxiety.
- Pay attention to feelings of fear and get to the root.

Chapter 5: Love
- God is love and doesn't want us to suffer.
- Cook with love.
- Worship out of love for God.

Chapter 6: Purity
- It's stupid to fill your mind with junk. It's like poison.
- Drink water and exercise.
- Cut unholy soul ties.

Chapter 7: Father, Son, and Holy Spirit.
- We must have a right view of God the Father.
- Jesus knew that the real struggle was against the powers of darkness.
- We must live full of the Holy Spirit to live the balanced life.

Hi, there. I wanted to introduce myself to you. My name is Melissa Gray, but my friends call me Mel. I just want you to know I am a regular person. I'm not famous, or a pastor of a big church. I'm not brilliant or a philosopher. I'm just someone who has been following Jesus for most of my fifty-two years on this earth. My biggest accomplishment is being the mother of six amazing children, and it is for those children and all of you that I wanted to write this book. My true passion is to see all people healed and whole, balanced, and truly happy. This book will be a story of how a regular person has found peace, healing, and balance in the midst of busyness, suffering, and just the mundane schedule of everyday living. How do we maintain peace when the hardships come? How do we thrive even when circumstances don't cooperate? How do we develop a relationship with God when we are so busy? These and other questions will be explored throughout this book, and I truly hope you enjoy reading and taking this journey with me. I need to mention as well that the stories used in this book have been used with permission. Names and details have been changed to maintain privacy where needed.

CHAPTER

Creating Awareness

As we begin our journey into balance, each chapter will have a section on the mind, body, and soul, all with an emphasis on one subject. It may seem a bit awkward at first to jump from the awareness of the mind to our body and then to the soul, but once we begin to see the pattern, hopefully it will begin to flow. Often we tend to focus more naturally on one area of balance. If we are mostly a logical type person, the mind will be a comfortable place to develop and strengthen. If we are more of a feeler, then perhaps the concept of the soul may be where we feel naturally secure. My hope is that by focusing on mind, body, and soul while tackling each specific subject, anything that is out of balance will become highlighted, and therefore a shift will begin to take place to bring back harmony, so all three parts of our being can function together as one. Let's begin.

The Mind
I'm smiling right now while thinking about how the subject of balance relates to awareness, because the question is,

how can we be aware of something that we are unaware of? As we begin to explore this topic as it relates to the mind, body, and soul, we will discover together the areas where we have been unaware and how this can affect us.

Do you remember the commercial from the '70s that coined the iconic saying "The mind is a terrible thing to waste"? This slogan has become part of the American vernacular because it is so very true. Norman Vincent Peale says in one of his famous quotes, "Our happiness depends on the habit of mind we cultivate." Often, however, there is a lack of awareness of and even honesty about our actual thoughts. Therefore, we can't even begin to cultivate the happiness we long for. Unconsciously our minds can repeat, "I'm not good enough. I'm a loser. I'll never amount to anything. I'll never be able to achieve that." These thoughts can begin to define us while we remain unaware it's even happening. Worse yet, maybe there is a feeling of being trapped in shameful thought patterns, hoping that no one will ever find out what really goes on inside our minds. These thoughts have become so familiar that they have almost become like a dull noise in our heads defining our very identity. Finally, we may be so used to the numbing noise of life that we have forgotten about our dreams and passions, therefore missing what God might be trying to tell us.

So how do we begin to become aware of the thoughts that may be unconsciously shaping our identity? The simple answer is, begin to pay attention to your thoughts. I have to admit, this does not come easily to me. I'm what my friends call a free spirit. This can be good because I like to have fun, but sometimes I need to force myself to go deeper and pay attention so I don't miss the important messages for life's direction. Curt Thompson says we need to begin to pay attention to what we're paying attention to. Notice where our minds wander when we are relaxed. What are we thinking about? What are the things we dwell on while driving or resting? Are we thinking about a relationship, a situation, family, a memory? What is taking up our brain space? During these moments, I catch myself and ask, "What was that thought in my head?" Sometimes these thoughts are funny or entertaining, like, "Why do the trees bounce up and down while I walk?" Other times they can be negative like, "I'm not good enough or smart enough," or "I'm happy my friend failed. Now I feel better about myself." Yikes! At this point, we need to know there is an invitation waiting for us to ask Jesus to become a part of the conversation in our heads. It's important to ask, why would I think that? Is it true? Where is that thought coming from? This technique begins to create awareness. It's paying attention to what we're paying attention to. Then we can begin to talk to God about these thoughts, rather than leaving them swirling around in our heads, defining who we are without our even realizing it's happening.

Let me give an example. One Sunday at church we had a guest speaker, my dear friend Dr. Martin Sanders. He said that sometimes people have thoughts that go something like this, "You are so dumb. You will never amount to anything. You're ugly. You are a loser." Some were surprised that people had such thoughts and others felt as though he were talking directly to them. They asked, "Were you talking to me? Those are the thoughts that run in my head?" These dear ones had been tortured for many years with old tapes playing in their minds, and they didn't know how to get free. They had become so used to these thoughts that they believed them and almost didn't even realize there was a different way to think. I'm not saying that these are your exact thoughts, but what I am asking is, what is the dialogue running through your mind? What are you thinking? Where does your mind wander when you are alone? Just begin to pay attention.

It is so it important to have a clear picture and awareness of exactly what we are thinking and to not block out our thoughts with distraction. Cell phones, computers, and unlimited entertainment make this extremely hard, but when we stay unaware, it is then that negative thought patterns can influence us without our permission. God's word, however, gives us another alternative. Philippians 4:8–9 says,

> Whatever is true, whatever is honorable, whatever is just, whatever is pure, whatever is lovely, whatever is commendable, if there is any excellence, if there is anything worthy of praise, think about these things. What you have learned and received and heard and seen in me, practice these things, and the God of peace will be with you.

Paul is emphasizing that what we think matters. He says that if we make a choice to begin to think about the good, then the God of peace will be with us, and our thoughts will actually have a direct effect on the level of peace we experience, but this requires us to pay attention. We must realize that balance starts in the mind. We need to be aware of what we are thinking and ask ourselves questions like, "What am I thinking about? Do I really need to focus on the negative regarding that person or situation?" We must remember that the thoughts we think will have a direct impact on the balance we experience in life. We will begin to realize that some of the things we think are toxic and poisonous, throwing off our sense of peace. To become whole, balanced, and free, we must begin to pay attention to which thoughts are true, good, and beneficial and which thoughts are destructive, negative, and detrimental.

Throughout the book I will share stories with permission. Please note that where needed, names and details have been changed to protect privacy. Stories are so important as we discuss this topic because they inspire and teach us how others have discovered to live balanced lives. Because I have had the privilege to guide hundreds of people into a journey of healing and wholeness, I have been able to see what works to achieve a life of balance and freedom. I have had failures and victories, but through it all, I can say my passion is to see the world healed and whole.

Story number one: Pamela came to me for prayer because she heard I might be able to help her understand why she was so angry. She was angry at her husband, depressed, and thinking of ending her marriage. She felt he was neglectful and distant. The type of prayer I guide people in is a listening form of prayer, so we started to listen in silence for a few minutes. Sometimes people are afraid they won't hear anything, but I have never had one person in twenty years not hear from God. So while Pam and I were praying, God began to reveal to her that He loved her and was proud of her. God highlighted her relationship with her dad and the feeling she had of never measuring up as a child. She had a memory of bringing home an A- on her report card and feeling rejected. As a result, she had become a perfectionist and had a hard time feeling like she was ever good enough. She then started to make others feel as if they were never measuring up, especially those close to her. Her husband became distant, not because he didn't love her but because he was tired of the feeling coming from her that he could never quite meet her expectations. She had thoughts in her mind that said, *You really could have done that better. Next time you will do a better job. You didn't get it quite right. You are really not that great.* She didn't think anything of these thoughts because that was how she was raised. She was so used to the running dialogue in her head that told her she wasn't good enough that she didn't realize the damage these thought patterns were actually having in her life and in the lives of the people she loved. When she discovered the reason behind these feelings, she was set free. Do you see why it is important to be aware and purposeful about how we think? Without it, we are walking through life with a blindfold on, potentially hurting those we love the most.

So, how do we begin this journey into awareness? It starts by paying attention to our thoughts, the ones that seem harmless enough, all the way to the negative, ugly, violent, and shameful ones in our minds. This can be a scary place because of the uncertainty of the nagging question, "What if the thoughts are really true? What if I really am defined by the thoughts I am thinking?" Perhaps we keep suppressing, we keep running, we keep turning away, but the thoughts are still there, popping up at the strangest and most inconvenient times. Instead, let the thoughts come from the mundane to the ugly, and then begin to talk to Jesus about them. He is not embarrassed or shocked by what you are thinking. Ask Him why these thoughts are in your head, and from where they originated. It is only in this brave act of coming to Jesus just as we are that true freedom and healing can come.

We often have guests over for dinner or dessert. I make sure that the downstairs, kitchen, living room, and dining room look great, organized, and clean. Upstairs, though, can be a very different story. With six children and two large dogs, there are usually piles of laundry, closets overflowing with clutter, and dirty bathrooms. Wouldn't it be foolish to leave the upstairs dirty because I chose to ignore it or refused to ask for help to clean it if needed? Our minds can be like this, full of clutter and darkness. Jesus is waiting at the door of our minds to come in, clean, and heal the messy thoughts inside us. He wants to take these embarrassing thoughts that we have been hiding and turn them into something beautiful. Instead of hiding, distracting ourselves, or pretending, it's time to bring our thoughts to God.

We will begin to explore many aspects of living in balance and staying in balance throughout this book, but for now, let's just focus on paying attention. What are the thoughts that are filling your mind? As you become more aware, you can begin to bring them to God through prayer. As you begin to talk to God about your thoughts, you will feel your mind become balanced and calm.

The Body

Now let's come out of the deep waters for a few minutes and discuss awareness as it relates to the body. This may seem odd at first, because discussions about health can sometimes feel shallow compared to exploring the soul and the mind, but please trust me that without including this section on the body, we are leaving out a very important aspect of balance. Many powerful leaders have been derailed in life because they didn't know how to rest, eat, play, sleep, and exercise. We will spend time navigating these topics as well because without our health … Well, you can finish that sentence. So let's jump in and focus on the body, eating, resting, and paying attention to our physical selves for a few minutes.

There are many ways we could navigate this next topic, but for now, the focus will be on paying attention to what we eat and why. I have to admit, I used to be a junk food gourmet living on diet soda and food from a box. After all, don't Swedish fish come from Sweden? Seriously though, it wasn't until my husband started getting migraine headaches almost every day that I knew we had to make a change. Brillat-Savarin coined the phrase, "You are what you eat." I have found this to be so very true. When I eat junk, I feel like junk. When I eat clean, I feel energetic and alive. What we put into our bodies can have a profound effect on our overall sense of well-being. So, just as we have begun to focus on awareness in the mind, let's begin to cultivate an awareness of what we are eating, so we can be and stay balanced.

So often, we eat mindlessly, unaware of what and why we are eating. Let me illustrate by this example. One friend recently told me she had to train herself to ask, "Why am I eating this?" Instead of just unconsciously eating a whole container of cookies, she started to stop and say, "What is the reason behind this eating?" Sometimes she was just eating to numb a wound. Other times it was more about rebellion, or it just felt good to eat the sugar. It wasn't until she stopped to ask this question, and to be honest with herself, that she began to gain control over the impulsive behavior and mindless eating.

The first step to healthy eating is honesty. Can we get honest and say, "I'm going to eat this whole pizza right now because I think it will make me feel good"? I am gaining my comfort from this pizza, nice pizza, loving pizza, kind pizza! We are like the cookie monster from Sesame Street gobbling our food down without a thought as to *why*. As we begin to pay attention to our motives, God can come in and begin to bring us real peace and healing—one that will last and not fade away after the last cookie is gone.

Why is it important to pay attention as we eat, instead of just shoving food down our throats without a thought about it? Because without a healthy diet, the balance of our lives can quickly be toppled. I have experienced this firsthand by eating too much sugar. I can go through a whole pint of coffee ice cream without even thinking about it, and the next day have a horrible sugar hangover and a headache and feel exhausted. So, even though my mind and soul may be very balanced and spiritual, if my body is out of whack, everything in my life suffers. I'm not saying I never eat coffee ice cream, but I try and balance my diet with about 90% good food and 10% everything else..

To maintain a balanced life, we must begin to practice mindful eating. Notice I said mindful, not obsessive. Just begin to pay attention to what you are eating and why. We will explore healthy ways to eat and approach food in each chapter, but it all begins with honesty and awareness. My husband and I were forced to start paying attention because we started to feel so crummy. We found our *why*, that thing that motivated us to make a change. What is your *why*? What is a big enough reason for you to make a change? Don't let yourself end up overweight, sick, miserable, and exhausted and say, "How did this happen?" Begin to pay attention to what and why you are eating. This is the first step to living a balanced and happy life.

The Soul

Finally, let's focus on the soul, the third part in our triad of balance. What is the soul? I like to think of the soul as that part of us that makes us, us. Some people call it the heart or that deep place where we experience emotion. It is our core identity and is unique to each one of us. Awareness as it relates to the soul can seem mysterious, but let's begin to explore it together.

Dr. Rob Reimer says in his book, *Soul Care*,

> You've heard the expression: What you don't know won't hurt you. But when it comes to the soul, that is a dangerous lie. What you don't know is already killing you. Just as we need awareness in our minds and our bodies, we need to pursue awareness in our souls. ... We cannot heal that which we will not admit. God cannot cleanse that which we will not confess.

This takes great courage because oftentimes we are ashamed of these dark places of the soul. Perhaps we don't want to admit there is a problem, or maybe the pain is buried so deep that we try to pretend there is nothing wrong. Pretending, though, will not bring freedom. It's time to bring into the light what we have been hiding, for freedom to be active in our lives.

I recently wrote a song called "All to You." The first line in the song says, "Shine your light, shine your light in my heart. No more dark, no more dark in my heart." I wrote it because sometimes we need God's help bringing to the light the things that are causing the imbalance. We cannot become fully healed and restored until we allow the Holy Spirit to shine His light into those dark places we have been running from, or have been unaware. Have you ever stubbed your toe because you couldn't see where you were going? It's the worst! You needed a light to highlight that piece of furniture so you could avoid bumping into it. This is what Jesus does for us if we ask Him.

I remember vividly praying with my dear friend when I had one of those moments of clarity. She asked to pray with me because she felt something was weighing me down. I told her I felt fine, but if she wanted to pray, I wouldn't stop her. Honestly, I was being kind of a brat, thinking I was just fine, thank you very much! But after just a few moments of prayer, where we invited Jesus to shine His light, it became highlighted to me that I was holding on to unforgiveness. I was astonished! I had no idea that unforgiveness was inside of me, but God knew and wanted me to be free. This is what God's Spirit will do for us if we ask Him. He will be the light that shines into those dark places so we won't become weighed down and out of balance by what we can't see.

So where do we begin as we think about balancing the soul? The first step is to ask God to begin to shine His light and to highlight where we need healing. This takes patience and courage. It can be scary to become soul aware, because sometimes it's painful. But please know that it is worth it. Even when we don't like what we see, we cannot begin to experience balance without looking at those hard places and facing them with openness and honesty. Begin to pay attention to what God highlights and just start a conversation. Maybe you like to write down your thoughts and prayers. Maybe you need to process by talking to Him out loud. Whatever it takes to start a dialogue with God, this will be your key to balance and freedom—paying attention to what Jesus highlights and then talking to Him about it. This is the rhythm of balance.

Just as we must begin paying attention to the conversations we are having with ourselves, I must touch on the importance of paying attention to our dreams and passions as well. What makes you excited? What injustices make you angry? What kind of people or people groups are you drawn to? The answers to these questions could also be the key to what you might be called to do with your life. God wires each of us with unique passions, but sometimes we are being pushed into a mold by the world and we miss what we are really supposed to be doing. I will never forget the day I was sitting with a group of my friends, and we decided to have a quiet time where we could focus on our dreams and desires. Out of that two-hour meditation, one of my friends realized that her lifelong concern for single mothers and their unborn babies was leading her to open up a home for them. Simply by paying attention to her passions, she realized her calling. How are you uniquely wired? What do you think and care about? Pay attention. You might be called to change the world.

Before we tackle the next area regarding the lies in our lives and how these lies can throw us off balance, I would like to take a few minutes to put what we have just read into action. At the end of each chapter, there will be a "Balance Sheet" section. This is an opportunity to put our balance principles into action. Please, do not just read these suggestions but do them, practice them, experiment, and have fun! Maybe put them up on the refrigerator, or do the sheets in community. Find a friend or two and try living your balance together. It is so important to not be just an observer but a participant while walking on the road to balance.

Balance Sheet For Awareness

Mind

Pay attention to what you are paying attention to. This week take a few minutes per day to focus on what thoughts are running in your head. Are they positive or negative? Write them down. If they are negative, begin to ask God where they are coming from and if He has something different to say about you or to you. Remember, His voice is not condemning or demeaning. So, be aware. Pay attention to your thoughts. Don't become discouraged if you don't hear anything from God. This is just the beginning of the journey. If you want to take this further, a great tool for this awareness journey is called Enneagram. You can take the test online at the website wepss.com.

Body

This week write down everything you eat and drink. Maybe, go one step further and write down why you are eating and drinking certain things. Don't judge. Just begin to notice. Find your *why*. Why am I eating and drinking certain things? Why do I want to make a change?

Soul

Take a few minutes and ask God to shine His light into your soul and to reveal anything He wants to show you. Notice what becomes highlighted. Then ask Him why He showed this to you and what He wants you to know. Maybe start a journal. Again, be patient with yourself. Don't judge. Just begin this two-way conversation with God. You may be surprised that God has been talking to you already, but you just didn't realize it was Him.

Thank you Meg Kempton for the Balance Sheet idea.

CHAPTER 2

Truth vs Lies

The Mind

Do you ever feel inadequate? Do you ever think that others are better than you, or more valuable than you? Do you compare yourself with others? Do you struggle with jealousy, anxiety, or feelings of insecurity? Do you get offended or discouraged easily? If you answered yes, chances are, you are believing a lie.

Lies can be very sly creatures. They are tricky because often, we don't even realize we are believing a lie. We feel something about ourselves, or about another person, and we think that what we believe is the truth. In fact, we have been living with this thought or idea for so long that it has become part of us. This belief in many ways defines our identity. Take for instance the young girl who grows up with a mom who is not very loving or kind. The mom rarely tells the little girl that she is loved and treasured. In fact, the girl often feels like she is just a bother to her mom. She feels that she is in the way, rather than loved and cherished. A lie begins to take root in the girl's heart.

17

The lie says, "You are not really that valuable. You are not smart or pretty or all that special."

The little girl grows into a teenager and adult. She becomes a super achiever to try to counteract the lie that plagues her. She gets straight A's, plays the piano with excellence, gets into a great college, has a boyfriend, and graduates with honors. She has everything going for her, yet she never feels like she is good enough. She always feels like there is something missing and begins to project this feeling onto her boyfriend and her close friends. She might say something like that they are never there for her or that they are constantly letting her down. They can never seem to quite measure up. The truth is, the lie she is believing is ruling her life, and she doesn't even know it.

At this point I'd like to pause and share with all the moms reading this book how to be the greatest mom ever. Are you ready! Love your children through nurture. Hug them. Say you're sorry when you blow it. Look into their eyes and empathize with their feelings. That's it. I promise. Your role as mom is to love. You can mess up a lot of things, but if you express love through nurture, your kids will experience the balance they need and grow up just fine. Dads, your free advice will be later. Okay, now back to the subject of our balance and how lies can throw us off.

What do you believe about yourself? Do you believe that you are worth the highest value? Do you believe that you were created to offer the world something unique, that only you can bring? Do you believe that you are loved, truly loved, not for what you do but simply for who you are? If you answered no to any of these questions, then perhaps you are believing a lie.

Remember the example of stubbing your toe in a pitch black room. Let's go back to that image for a moment. Remember, there is not one speck of light in the room. You can't see a thing. It's utter darkness. Then, you take out your flashlight and magically, you can see the room and everything in it. This concept is so important when asking God to expose the lies in our minds. Putting balance into action means taking the time to ask Jesus to shine His light into our minds and asking Him if there are any lies we are believing. When we do this, it is like taking out a flashlight and asking God to expose any lies that have been hiding in a dark corner. Often an idea becomes highlighted so we can conclude that this is a lie.

The word of God in Romans 12 tells us to renew our minds. How do we do this? After God begins to highlight a lie, we can begin by taking it to God and saying something like this: "Dear God, I am no longer agreeing with that lie. I receive the truth and the effects of the truth into my mind, body, and soul." This simple prayer shows us how we can come out of agreement with the lie and renew the mind. By simply stating we will no longer agree with the lie, we can begin to become free from all of the bondage this wrong belief has created in our lives.

Here is a lie I used to believe. One day I was in a time of prayer, and God revealed to me that I thought He was a God who liked to keep His distance. This lie stemmed from my childhood. My father was not an affectionate dad.

He was an alcoholic, and he was very distant emotionally. Therefore, I thought God the Father was a distant God who wasn't really interested in the details of my life. I have to say, this was a shock. I didn't realize I believed this about God until I sought Him about the lies in my life. Like that light shining in a dark room, the lie was exposed. So, I asked God to show his true self to me. He showed me a picture of a huge, loving Father, and I was sitting on His lap! He looked really happy and proud of me. This forever changed my view of myself and of my heavenly Father. Now, instead of feeling like God probably doesn't want to be bothered with the little problems in my life, I feel like my dear Papa can't wait to hear from me! He can't wait to hear about my day and anything else I want to tell Him.

Do you see how believing one simple lie can change the course of a life and the lives around you? Nancy Leigh DeMoss says in her book, *The Lies Women Believe*, "The important thing to remember is that every act of sin in our lives begins with a lie. We listen to the lie; we dwell on it until we believe it; finally, we act on it." This is profound! We don't need to settle for believing lies. Instead, we can believe the truth that we are each perfectly and wonderfully made by a loving heavenly Father. We can renew our minds with truth about who God says we are, not who the world says we are. Psalm 139 says, "For you formed my inward parts; you knitted me together in my mother's womb. I praise you, for I am fearfully and wonderfully made. Wonderful are your works; my soul knows it very well." Let's focus on this truth together until we begin to really believe it—until those old tapes in our heads are replaced by new words uniquely crafted for us by God our Creator. As we do this, we will feel a balance enter our minds and a strength pouring into our lives.

The Body

Okay, let's switch gears and focus on the lies that relate to our bodies for a few moments. Again, switching from lies of the mind to lies of the body may feel abrupt and somewhat awkward, but truly, lies of the body can throw us off balance just as quickly as lies of the soul. There are so many lies in our society about the body that it is hard to even begin to tackle this topic, but let's start with lies about food because it is food that has a profound effect on the balance we experience. We are bombarded with the media telling us that certain foods are good for us. We are told if we eat more meat, we will be healthy. No, wait! If we eat more carbs, then we will be healthy. No, wait again! The secret is eating an all-vegetable diet. Oh brother! What is true? Maybe there is another lie that you tell yourself, that eating a healthy diet is too hard or doesn't really matter all that much. After all, as long as I read the Bible and love others, isn't that enough? Does it really matter what I eat? I feel pretty good. Perhaps this is true, but let's go back to where it all started and unpack some lies together in the garden of Eden.

I find it absolutely fascinating that the first time we encounter deception in the Bible, it's regarding what is good to eat and what is not. Genesis 3:6 says, "So when the woman saw that the tree was good for food, and that it was a delight to the eyes, and that the tree was to be

21

desired to make one wise, she took of its fruit and ate, and she also gave some to her husband who was with her, and he ate." God told her not to eat of the tree, but perhaps she told herself a lie that went something like this: "No, it will be fine if I eat this fruit. In fact, it will be good for me." Hmmmm. How does the woman disobey a direct command from God and yet convince herself that it will all be good? The answer could be that she was believing a lie.

Let's go a bit further in our discussion of the passage. Isn't it interesting that the first commandment God gave the man and woman was about food? He said," You can eat of all these plants I made, but of this one tree, don't eat it." Curious, isn't it? God told the man and woman that the food from a certain tree would not be good for them. He could have used any object to illustrate His point, but He chose food. Of course, the choice of eating from the tree of good and evil goes way beyond a discussion about food, and there are deep and complex issues that could fill a whole book on this one topic alone, but for the sake of our focus, one of the things we can conclude is that God does care about what we eat and what we don't eat. Clearly, God says that one tree is good to eat from, and the other is not. Perhaps the same principle is true for us, that some foods are good to eat and others are not. It really does matter the type of food we eat, and if we want to live a balanced life, we must begin to come out of agreement with the lie that, *I can eat whatever I want and not be affected.*

Just like Eve, we too can believe the lie that it will be fine if we eat the forbidden fruit. The lies that we tell ourselves can go something like this: "It will be fine if I eat this whole pint of ice cream. I'll feel better after I eat this whole bag of cookies. Tomorrow I will start to eat better." On and on it goes. We can trick ourselves into thinking that food will bring us comfort or that it doesn't really matter what we eat. The woman deceived herself, saying, "God did not really tell me to not eat this food." What a lie! Eating that food cost her eternal life. It cost her fellowship with God. It brought her death. Maybe take a moment and ask, "Are there any ways I'm deceiving myself when it comes to food? Have I convinced myself that the sugar high will make me feel better? Have I told myself that it doesn't really matter what I put into my body and that I don't want to turn into one of those health nuts anyway? Have I believed the lie that it's just too hard, that I don't have the time, that I'm too far gone?" These are all lies from an enemy who wants to destroy you.

So, the big question is where do we begin? There are so many choices, diets, and books. How do we even know what it means to eat "healthy"? It's actually not as complicated as the world makes it out to be. If we simply begin this journey by trying to eat as much whole food as possible, we are off to a good start. Whole foods are vegetables, fruits, nuts, seeds, meat, healthy fats like olive oil, whole grains like brown rice and quinoa, foods that are closest to their original created form. It's really that simple!

So, simply begin by thinking about what you are putting into your mouth and why. Are you eating food to medicate your pain or out of boredom? Why are you eating what you're eating? Is there a lie you are believing about food? As we begin to think about the answers to these questions, we will be taking a huge first step. For some of us, the unhealthy ways we eat are actually an addiction. For others, we just haven't really thought about how we eat and how it can affect our overall balance. When we eat whole foods, our bodies will be able to function the way God created them to. We will feel the symmetry of balance instead of the highs and lows of a caffeine buzz or sugar coma. We can be the most spiritual people on earth, but if we are eating an unhealthy diet, there will be a lack of balance and energy.

Maybe take a few minutes now and think about your diet. How can you begin to make small changes and start to eat food the way God originally made it to be? Remember, the farther away a food is from its original state, the harder it is for your body to digest. You can do this! Begin to bring your body into balance so you can live life to the fullest.

The Soul
Finally, let's jump back into that deep water and talk about the lies of the soul. Hopefully by now you are used to this pattern and it won't feel too abrupt. Truthfully, because I tend to get bored easily, part of me hopes the changes of topic will interest you enough to keep you reading to the end of the book. So, let's continue on the journey of the lies of the soul. One could say that the ultimate lie of the soul is shame. Shame says you are not enough. You are not good enough, smart enough, pretty enough, or handsome enough. This outlook can lead us to do crazy, destructive

things to ourselves and others. If the belief is that I am lacking, then I will look to fill or medicate the pain of that feeling in any way that I can.

Many years ago, I received training to pray for people who wanted emotional healing. We were taught to help them listen and respond to God. Since then, I have had the privilege to pray with hundreds of people and to be a part of their freedom journey. On one such day, Mr. J came to me for a healing prayer appointment. He had been having an affair and felt very unsatisfied in his marriage. He had several small children and felt they occupied most of his wife's attention and focus and was thinking of leaving her. During the prayer time, he realized that he never felt good enough as a child. His father didn't believe in giving praise or affirmation, so he felt that no matter what he did, he didn't measure up. Deep in his soul he felt shame. He felt that he wasn't enough. So, when his wife became distracted or she was tired, he took it as personal rejection and started looking elsewhere to fill the hole. He started sneaking around, lying, and deceiving himself and his family.

Curt Thompson in his book *Soul of Shame* says,

> Unfortunately, this invariably leads to the isolation of hiding from ourselves, from each other and from God, continuing to make up our stories on our own, terrified of collaborating in the telling of stories with others for fear that our nakedness will be revealed and exploited. The eventual, inevitable outcome of this isolation is

> hell … It is the counter echo of God's
> mandate that it is not good to be alone.
> Shame's power lies in its subtlety and
> silence … and is quite content to remain
> in its self-perpetuating cycle of judgment
> and hiding. (pp. 113–114)

Shame says, "If I hide then I will be okay. I won't tell anyone my struggle and won't tell what I am doing in the dark. If they find out my secret, I will be ruined, humiliated, rejected." It says, "After I eat the forbidden fruit, I must run and hide. Hide from God. Hide from others. Cover my secret and never let anyone know about it." However, there is a big problem with this strategy. In hiding our secret sin, the shame is allowed to grow and fester, and a poisonous lie is created. There is this tension of wanting to keep our shame in the dark and yet realizing that shame needs the dark to grow.

I remember going to camp one summer on Martha's Vineyard. The camp had a gardener who tended the grounds. One day he brought a rather large box with a tent over it. He said that there were bean sprouts growing inside the tent and that they grew better in the dark. I took a peek at the sprouts, and to be honest I was not impressed. The gardener said, "I just picked a bunch of the sprouts, but come back first thing in the morning and take a look." Well, I was curious. So, the next morning I peeked into the box and was actually kind of creeped out. The sprouts were like little aliens that had filled the box literally overnight.

Shame is like those sprouts; it grows best in the dark. The lie says, "Don't tell anyone your struggle. Don't talk to God about it." The truth is, however, that when you share it, the hold that a particular sin has on your life will be broken. It takes the greatest courage to talk about the abuse that happened to us, the pornography addiction, the gender confusion, the affair, the jealousy, the hatred. I encourage you, dear one. Find a trusted friend, a pastor, a family member, and begin the journey of sharing your secrets. Most importantly, talk to God about your secrets. As you share those secrets, the power of the lie will be broken. This has been true in my life. I had been hiding a secret. Finally, when I confessed it to a trusted friend, I was free! It literally was that simple. I had agonized about sharing this secret. I thought I could conquer it on my own, but I still struggled. Finally, when I shared it with my husband and best friend, the power was broken, and I was completely free. I was shocked at how easy it was to break the power that this secret had over me.

Another gentleman who had struggled with the secret of attending strip clubs took a very hard step and confessed this to his wife. He was set free and hasn't returned to one of these places since. Please hear me when I say this is not easy. There may even be some fall out from your confession, especially if it hurts those you are confessing to. But I guess the question is, do you want to be free? If you do, then bring your secret to a trusted friend and come clean.

Finally, and most importantly, share your secrets with God. Don't run away from Him. After all, He knows already. He longs for you to come and talk to Him about it. He longs to know how you feel. You say to yourself, "I could never talk to God about my pornography addiction, or the abuse I suffered as a child or the thoughts I'm having." Why of course you can! You can talk to God about anything. He is your loving Father. Run to Him. As the Steffany Gretzinger song says, "Come out of hiding, you're safe here with me." You are safe with your heavenly Father. It's time. The balance you long for is right in front of you. Take action. Break the lies. You won't regret it.

Balance Sheet for Lies

Mind

Take a few minutes and ask God if there are any lies you are believing about yourself or God. If anything comes to your mind, ask God what the truth is. Take a few minutes to come out of agreement with the lie and to embrace the truth. You can say something like this: "I no longer agree with this lie. I receive the truth instead." Try to be as specific as possible. This can be done as often as necessary.

Body

Think about the foods you are eating that are processed and full of sugar. Slowly start to replace these foods with whole foods. Begin to write down why you are eating certain foods. Think about if you are eating out of stress, and write down other ways to deal with stress or sadness.

Soul

Begin to talk to God about your secret shame. Then find a trusted friend or two who will listen to a life confession, where you begin to share the secrets that you have never shared with anyone. Pray for each other. You can practice confession on a regular basis.

CHAPTER 3

Forgiveness

The Mind

I have spoken to people who truly believe that forgiveness is equivalent to a four-letter word. How can I forgive a person who abused me, who deceived me, who hurt someone I love, who is just plain evil? I get it. Forgiveness is not for the cowardly or weak minded. However, maybe we have believed a false definition of forgiveness, and this has stopped us from even considering the release of our own bitterness. Forgiveness does not mean that I am excusing the person who did the horrible thing to me. I am not saying that it is fine for the abuser to abuse, for the murderer to murder, for the adulterer to commit adultery. Please hear this. Forgiveness simply means making a choice to give that person and their punishment to God. It means that I make a choice to let God be the one to bring about justice. It is a choice to allow God to be the judge and the jury. It takes great courage to begin to wade into the waters of forgiveness, but it is a journey worth exploring if we truly want to feel whole and balanced. It also takes great faith. We have to trust that God is the greatest equalizer and that letting go of our hurt and desire for revenge will actually be better for us.

So the question is, do we want to be set free? We must pause and evaluate whether it will be worth it. Is it worth the time and emotional energy? I want to propose, yes! When we carry unforgiveness, it is like holding a set of heavy chains that bind us up and weigh us down. I'm making a strong argument in favor of forgiveness because our view about this subject could be the very key that brings us into balance. If we believe it's worth it, we will have the courage to go to the hard places that lead to freedom. If we don't, then we just won't do it. It's that simple. I heard a wise saying once that goes like this: unforgiveness is like drinking poison and expecting the other person to die. The truth is, it can be difficult to go back to the painful memories, but the pain will only last a moment compared to the freedom that will last a lifetime. It is definitely worth taking the time necessary to release all unforgiveness so we are not poisoning ourselves.

So, like I stated before, it all begins with our thinking. Once we get to the place of belief that our bitterness is weighing us down and needs to go, then we can begin the process of forgiving. Here is a simple method I have used for years. First, begin by saying: "Lord, I choose to forgive (name the person) for (name the specific thing). I release this person to you and I bless them through the power of Jesus name." I really like this particular prayer because it uses the word, choose. When we realize that we have the right to choose forgiveness, it is empowering. To choose forgiveness engages our will. It is a process that begins with a thought and ends in an action.

The forgiveness prayer may need to be prayed many times throughout our lives, as we want to make sure we are never holding on to bitterness or anger for long periods of time. This process may need to be repeated several times before the actual feeling of forgiveness comes, but don't give up. The sweet feeling of forgiveness will come in time. The length of time may depend on the depth of the wound, but keep pressing in, because this is a major key to living a balanced life.

If you find you are stuck or are unsure if you are really letting go of your unforgiveness, here is another strategy. Begin by asking someone to pray your prayer out loud with you. I've found that the spoken word can be more effective than merely keeping the declaration in my head. After all, in Genesis 1, God spoke the world into existence. God could have thought the world and made it so, but instead, He spoke it, and it was so. There is great power and freedom in speaking the declaration of forgiveness out loud. If we speak curses about the person, bitterness and resentment will take root in our own hearts and minds. If we speak forgiveness and blessing, we ourselves will experience forgiveness and blessing. There is something very powerful that transpires in our own lives as we declare forgiveness using the spoken word.

In Matthew 6, Jesus gives us the guidelines on how we should pray. He says we should ask God to forgive us the way we forgive others. This is sobering when we really think about it. Do I really want God to forgive me the way I forgive others? If we cannot answer yes, then we probably need to do the hard work of forgiveness. This prayer suggests that if we want to receive the full blessing of God's forgiveness in our own lives, then we must fully forgive those who have hurt us. For us to be set free, we must release our bitterness and give the offender to God.

I hope you are convinced how important active forgiveness is in maintaining the balance in your life. If you want freedom and fullness of joy, then practicing forgiveness needs to be a regular part of our life experience. This is a challenge because people can hurt us deeply. But I ask you, "Do you really want freedom? Do you really want joy? Do you really want to feel balanced?" If the answer is yes, then be courageous and begin to walk in active forgiveness.

The Body

Sometimes we think of ourselves as separate pieces, mind, body, and soul, that act independently of each other. This could not be further from the truth. There is actually a profound connection between the three. Each one affects the other. The truth is, our mortal bodies are deeply impacted by any bitterness we hold onto in our minds and in our souls. In his book *A More Excellent Way*, Pastor Henry Wright illustrates by saying,

> I consider all healing of spiritually rooted disease to be a factor of sanctification. I believe that all disease that has a spiritual root is a result of lack of sanctification in our

> lives as men and women of God. I believe
> all healing of disease and or prevention is
> the process of being re-sanctified. (p.91)

Sanctification is a fancy way of describing the process of becoming more like Jesus every day. When we receive the gift of forgiveness, our spirit is immediately made completely clean, but our flesh is still in process. There is a beautiful mystery and a tension in this thought, because on the one hand we can say, "I am not defined by sin, nor shall I even be called a sinner." Yet on the other hand, we know that our sin nature does not just disappear. Rather, it is a journey of becoming more like Jesus one day at a time. The mystery is, we are a new creation and yet still a work in progress.

Let me share a beautiful story that shows the connection between body, mind, and soul. I remember vividly sitting in a training seminar on healing prayer. The speaker told a story I will never forget. He said that one day there was an older woman who had come for prayer for her arthritic hands. She was in such pain and her hands were so disfigured that she could hardly stand it. She had been to doctors, but there was really nothing they could do. So, the prayer team gathered around her, and one of the members felt the distinct impression that the woman needed to forgive someone in her life. She asked the woman if this made any sense. "Yes," the woman said. "My father abused me and my sister. I have never been able to forgive him." After a while in prayer, the woman became convinced that she needed to forgive her father. As she began to release the bitterness, her gnarled fingers began to straighten, and she was completely healed!

As we can see, the connection between mind, body, and soul is very real. Oftentimes we can forget that our bodies are not separate from our minds and souls. We think, *Oh, I have a cold, a cough, a headache, depression. I must go to the doctor and get medicine, and then I will feel better.* We forget that our bodies are connected to our minds and souls and that maybe there is a deeper issue lodged in a secret place that is actually at the root of the sickness.

Holding onto bitterness can affect our bodies in a very debilitating way, but we must walk delicately along this path, because we never want to point the finger at someone else and say, "You are sick because there is sin in your life." This is what the Pharisees did in John 9. They assumed that the blind man or his parents had sinned because he was blind. Jesus shut this line of thinking down quickly, and so must we. This is how I maneuver through this tricky area. I am super hard on myself and super easy on everybody else. If I am feeling sick, tired, or depressed or have a headache or a cough, I immediately ask God to examine my heart and my mind for unforgiveness or unconfessed sin. I assume it's there, unless God shows me otherwise. But if I see someone else's sickness, I move with compassion and tenderness. I want to gently help the person explore any possible areas of his or her life where sickness or disease might have been allowed to take root and grow, and if they don't ask, I don't offer!

I will never forget several years ago when I was experiencing a chronic cough. I had been coughing for about six weeks, and it was so annoying! Finally, I asked God about it. I heard the answer very clearly. I heard the word *pride* inside my mind. You see, I had always prided myself on how healthy I was. I would secretly look down on people who ate poorly or didn't eat like me. Truthfully, I feel embarrassed to even admit this now, but it was very true. In an instant, the Holy Spirit revealed that I was full of pride and I needed to repent. Ouch! At that moment, I humbled myself and acknowledged how I had looked down on God's precious children. I told Him that I was sorry for my lack of love and owned that He was the one who kept me healthy. I acknowledged that He was far more concerned about my heart than what I put into my mouth. Guess what! The next day my cough was gone! This truly astonished me. Never again would I separate my body from my mind and soul. I realized that the three are mysteriously and beautifully connected, like a mobile. There are three strings equally balanced, with mind, body, and soul on each end. When one of the strings is pulled, the other strings are pulled with it. When all are balanced, there is calm, stillness, and peace.

There is a wise saying that goes like this: "Remember, the body doesn't lie." Pay attention to your body. If you are tired for no reason, lethargic for days on end, or have a headache, cold, or even something more serious, maybe your body is trying to tell you something. Sometimes there are things that are so deep and so painful that we have suppressed them, just to survive. Sometimes, we have justified our own lack of forgiveness for so long that it has become a part of us, and our body is trying to tell us to get rid of it. This can be a scary journey, but it is one worth taking if your desire is to be healthy and whole. Take the journey. Ask the tough questions. Rid yourself of unforgiveness, and experience balance and healing in your body. It is amazing and so worth it.

The Soul
Perhaps the most difficult person to forgive is ourselves. This is forgiveness of the soul. We are able to forgive even the most horrible actions of others, but when it comes to ourselves, there may be a secret loathing and contempt that we just can't let go. Every time we think about that shameful memory, we want to run and hide. We will never tell another person what we did. Never! We will keep that horrible memory or those shameful thoughts locked in a secret place where no one will ever find them. After all, if anyone found out what we really did, what we really thought and struggled with, there would follow a most profound and painful rejection. We think to ourselves, *I could not withstand this kind of rejection. I cannot even stand myself. Why should I expect someone else to love me if they found out who I really was?*

These next examples are so painful that to put them in print is truly agonizing, but we must, in order to heal. The first is that of the countless women who have hidden in their souls a secret abortion. Dear ones, I grieve with you, cry with you, and hurt with you. I have had the privilege to walk on the journey of healing with many of you, and I want to say thank you for your trust and bravery. The other example is the men and women who were sexually abused as children. The shame of this abuse had lodged itself deep into their souls. Somehow, they couldn't forgive themselves for this abuse—as though it were their own fault. As though they were damaged goods and they were somehow to blame. These dear ones had forgiven the people who hurt them, but they could not forgive themselves. Perhaps the shame you carry is not quite so traumatic, but it plagues you nonetheless. The question is, how do we get rid of the shame of the soul? How do we forgive ourselves for the things we have done? The answer is in the cross of Jesus Christ.

I will never forget as a fourteen-year-old girl, sitting at a camp and reading Romans 5:8–9: "But God shows his love for us in that while we were yet still sinners, Christ died for us. Since, therefore we have now been justified by his blood, much more shall we be saved by him from the wrath of God." I was hit with the reality that Jesus Christ died on the cross and that *all* my sin was washed away by His blood. When God looked at me, He didn't see my shameful deeds, but He saw me as pure and holy. I was completely clean and new. So you too, dear one, are completely clean, holy, and new! Jesus took your sin to the cross with Him. He placed your sin upon Himself as though He were the one who had done the shameful things, not you. It is as though you never even did the act. You are completely new.

Sometimes I hear Christians say things like, "I am a miserable sinner." I understand why they say things like this, but I want to shout at them, "No, you are not! You are righteous and holy, totally clean, completely new." If we as Christians continue to define ourselves as miserable sinners, then it follows that we will behave as miserable sinners. My behavior will reflect what I think about myself. If, however, I see myself through the eyes of Christ, pure, blameless, and holy, I will instead act out of that identity. I heard a young lady say recently, "I would never date that guy. He just isn't good enough for me." I thought how very wise she was. She knew her value, so why would she settle for a man who was out there doing dumb and destructive things? She knew that she deserved better. She knew her worth. Do you know yours?

We must begin to press into this deep knowing of our own value. Can we begin to see ourselves, not as miserable sinners, but as those who are redeemed, forgiven, and righteous? Perhaps take a few minutes and ask your Father in heaven what He thinks about you. Ask Him how He feels about you. I think you will be pleasantly surprised that He thinks of you as His beloved son or daughter, righteous, pure, and holy, without stain or blemish. Let that truth sink deep into your soul. Let that define you. As the shame of the soul begins to be transferred to the cross of Christ, balance will come back into your life, and it will feel amazing!

Balance Sheet For Forgiveness

Mind

Take a few minutes and ask God, "Who do I need to forgive?" When someone comes to your mind, you can pray a prayer that goes something like this: "Dear Jesus, I choose to forgive this person. I release him or her to You and I bless him or her through the power of Your name." This prayer can be used on a regular basis throughout your life.

Body

Take a few minutes each day and breathe deeply. As you breathe, picture your lungs fill with air from the bottom to the top. As you exhale, empty from top to bottom. Begin to notice as you breathe if you have any pain in your body or any discomfort. Ask God if any of it is caused by unforgiveness or sin in your life. Turn your eyes to Jesus, and ask Him to help you forgive. Say out loud the forgiveness prayer. Give Jesus your anger, shame, guilt, and fear, and ask what He has for you in exchange. Then thank Jesus for His complete healing.

Soul

Have you forgiven yourself for your past? If not, hand over each area of shame one by one to Jesus. Ask Him to take your shame and to give you something different in return. What did Jesus give you instead? Pray the forgiveness prayer for yourself, and release blessings over yourself by saying, "I bless myself in Jesus's name." Meditate on 2 Corinthians 5:17. What is God showing you about who you are?

CHAPTER 4

Anxiety and Melancholy

The Mind

There is nothing that can throw off our balance faster than anxiety and melancholy. Did you know that what we think about actually changes the structure of the brain? I already knew about the importance of the focus of my thoughts, but I didn't realize that my brain could actually change in substance and function as a result of those thoughts. I believed that damage to the brain was mostly irreversible and that if people struggled with anxiety or depression, they were destined to struggle with this for the rest of their lives. In fact, scientists used to believe that the brain was unchangeable and that once damage was done, it could never be healed. However, research is now showing just the opposite. The brain is ever changing and reacting to our thoughts by forming new patterns and connections. Dr. Caroline Leaf in her book *Switch on Your Brain* says it like this:

> Taking this to a deeper level, research shows that DNA actually changes shape

> according to our thoughts. As you think
> those negative thoughts about the future,
> the week ahead, what a person might say
> or do, even in the absence of the concrete
> stimulus- that toxic thinking will change
> your brain wiring in a negative direction
> and throw your mind and body into stress.
> (p. 35)

This is absolutely fascinating. Conversely, as we choose to focus on the positive, our brains develop deep and lasting patterns of hope and the ability to endure hardship, without falling into despair.

One dear friend describes it like this: "After suffering with severe anxiety for years, I started to practice daily mindful meditation on the truths of God." As a result of this practice, she told me that her anxiety began to subside. When she started to feel the debilitating sense of fear start to come, she would quiet her mind by focusing on the truths of God, and slowly the feeling would subside. After practicing this for just several weeks, she noticed that after years of suffering, the frequency of the anxiety became less and less. Her brain was actually changing.

Along with meditation, I also recommend movement. I teach a form of exercise where each class begins with deep and focused breathing and stretching. I ask students when they breathe in to focus on God's love, and when they exhale, to let go of all stress. We do this for several minutes, until our racing thoughts slow down and we are able to feel a sense of calm. Then we begin to stretch and strengthen our bodies. You can practice this slow breathing by focusing on any truth that is meaningful to you. For instance, breathe in as you focus on "Father," and breathe out as you focus on, "I belong to You." Take any phrase and use it as your breathing prayer with God. Dr. Stacey Lemanski in her book *The Freedom Prayer Workbook* calls this "The Breath Prayer."

After practicing this kind of meditative prayer, you will notice that your anxiety will begin to decrease and the battle in your mind will become less intense. Those who have struggled with anxiety for years will tell you that they are slowly becoming free. Instead of their minds automatically going to debilitating anxiety, now their minds are starting to dwell on the faithfulness of God. The brain is actually rewiring itself.

The Bible says, "Do not be anxious about anything, but in everything by prayer and supplication with thanksgiving let your requests be made known to God. And the peace of God, which surpasses all understanding, will guard your hearts and your minds in Christ Jesus" (Philippians 4:6–7). The promise here is that as we focus on being thankful, we will experience peace. Isn't that amazing! Focused prayer is a kind of meditation that can turn our anxiety into thanksgiving. I actually wanted to see if this worked. The next time I was feeling anxious and crabby, I started to thank God for anything I could think of. Guess what happened? I started to feel better. I started to smile. I was amazed. God was telling the truth! I encourage you to try deep and meditative breathing and thankfulness. Let the power of God transform your brain and heal your anxiety. What we focus on will have a profound impact on the balance in our lives.

Now, let's take a few minutes to focus specifically on melancholy. Like anxiety, a deep sense of melancholy can quickly throw us off balance. Did you know that a sense of melancholy can affect the rich, the poor, the famous, and the powerful? Sometimes we think that if all our dreams come true, we'd finally be happy. We can think that if we had a certain amount of money or power, then we would feel good. This is an absolute lie! Think of the famous, wealthy, and powerful people who have fallen into complete despair. The truth is, worldly success does not bring happiness. My older brother shares in his testimony that when he finally "made it" and had money in the bank, his melancholy actually became worse. He says that at least when he was still striving to make the money that he thought would bring him happiness, he still had hope, but when he reached his dream of having it and still felt bad, the depression became much worse. We need to realize that happiness and fulfillment stem from something far different from where the world tells us they do. Our sense of well-being does not come from money, power, position, or fame, but it comes from knowing the person of Jesus Christ who is the way, the truth, and the life. It is only in knowing Jesus that my brother and countless others have been set free from depression and anxiety.

I remember one very vivid Sunday in church when my pastor, Doug Kempton, said to the congregation, "Jesus is the answer to all your problems." There was a reverent silence as we all pondered this statement. Could this really be true? Is Jesus the answer to depression, anxiety, fear, finances, and stress? The answer is yes! He truly is the answer to all of our problems. It is only in Jesus that we can live the balanced life and be set free from anxiety and melancholy.

I hope this does not seem overly simplistic in light of our complex life circumstances, but truly the answer to every problem is Jesus Christ. However, we tend to want to take control, blame others, and drown out the still, small voice of our Savior. Please, just slow down. Don't make that decision you are about to make. Wait! Seek Jesus and wait. Pray. Then wait some more. Slow down. Quiet the noise in your head by breathing deeply and inviting Jesus to guide you. Then wait again. Listen. Be still. Breathe. Balance.

The Body

It does make sense that what we think about can affect the level of our anxiety, but can anxiety be caused by what we put into our bodies as well? Is there a correlation between what I eat and the stress I feel? There was a fascinating study done by Dr. Bart Hoebel, professor of psychology and neuroscience at Princeton University. He found that rats that were given the choice between sugar and cocaine chose the sugar 94 percent of the time over the cocaine. As he studied their brains' response to sugar, he discovered that the rats became addicted to the sugar and suffered withdrawal symptoms when they didn't get it, as if they were addicted to drugs. This actually did not surprise me at all because I think we all know how addictive sugar can be! Furthermore, it was discovered that excessive sugar can actually be the cause of anxiety.

Here is a powerful example that my friend Stacey said I could share. She used to be addicted to sugar without even realizing it, because sugar was in most of the processed food she was eating. As she began to eat whole foods and less sugar, she noticed her brain fog beginning to clear. The combination of eating clean foods and the soul work she was doing began to change her life. Today, because she has detoxed from the sugar, even when she eats a little bit, she feels a crash in her body, fog in her brain, and aches in her joints. Sugar is truly toxic for her. You may not have such a dramatic reaction to sugar like Stacey, but perhaps it is messing with your balance more than you realize.

Let me take a minute to describe what actually happens when we eat processed sugar. First, we must realize that the body fights disease and sickness when the immune system is operating at 100 percent. Of course, that makes sense. Well, there are factors that cause the immune system to begin to break down. The major enemy of our immune system is inflammation. In fact, it has been discovered that sickness and disease flourish in an inflamed environment. Guess what? Sugar causes inflammation! So, that means when I eat sugar, I become more susceptible to sickness and disease. I don't know about you, but when I am sick, I am truly miserable and it throws off my balance.

So if sugar is one of the major causes of inflammation in our bodies, and if I am eating sugar regularly, I am potentially becoming more addicted, more inflamed, and more unable to fight disease and sickness every day. Furthermore, in 2002, a study of overall sugar consumption per person in six different countries (Canada, France, Germany, Korea, New Zealand, and the United States)—published by Dr. Arthur Westover, from the University of Texas Southwestern Medical Center in Dallas—implicated sugar as a factor in higher rates of major depression. So, not only does sugar make us more susceptible to sickness, but it has been linked to depression and anxiety as well.

I have to be honest with you. The studies are impressive, but really it just boils down to the fact that I hate being sick and feeling tired. If my sugar intake directly affects my immune system by causing inflammation, thereby making me more susceptible to becoming sick, then personally, it's worth it to me to cut way down on my sugar. It's that simple.

Unfortunately, sugar is the hidden ingredient in most processed foods. Anything that comes in a box, a can, or a wrapper most likely contains sugar. Therefore, I have become an avid label reader and try to eat mostly foods that are as close to the way God made them as possible.

I remember the day I cleaned out my pantry. I felt a bit guilty throwing away my boxes of processed food, my wrapped snacks, and my candy, but in the long run, it has been one of the best decisions of my life. Won't you give it a try? Do you even realize how much sugar you eat in a day? Do you know how much fake food are you eating? It's time to live a balanced life by taking care of the one body God has given you. You can do it!

The Soul

In one of my favorite movies of all time, *What About Bob*, there is a scene in the psychiatrist's office. Bob is talking to Dr. Marvin about his problems and he says, "I feel weird." Dr. Marvin responds with the words, "Talk about … weird." Let's spend the next few minutes talking about those "weird" feelings that drive us to take "weird" actions.

Why is it that we find ourselves acting irrationally? We know we are being childish, foolish, and unreasonable, but we can't help it. Why do we choose to binge watch television shows, drink too much, rage against those we love, and wallow in despair? Let me suggest that there is an unresolved soul issue and that these behaviors are actually a coping mechanism masking a deeper problem. Let me give an example. One day I was supposed to pick up my son from school after his sports practice. I got the time wrong and ended up being very late. I felt horrible. I started beating myself up about it. I got angry at myself. I couldn't let it go. It ruined my evening. How could I do this to my precious boy? Mind you, he wasn't affected at all. He got in the car and didn't even care that he had been waiting for a half hour. I knew I was being weird. What was really going on? Something was igniting my exaggerated response to a small situation. This is what is called a trigger. Something deeper was going on in my soul that needed healing. So finally, I asked God about it. I was brought back to my childhood. You see, my mother worked full time and I was often left places late or not picked up at all and had to walk. I remembered feeling abandoned and alone. A-ha! I was projecting my pain onto my son. There was a soul wound in my life that made my reaction way out of proportion to the actual situation.

I have learned to pay attention to these triggers and to actually welcome them because it means that there is an opportunity to receive healing. Perhaps when we are feeling anxious or weird, resorting to destructive behavior, or have a feeling of melancholy, there is something deeper going on. If we take a few minutes to talk to God about it and ask Him to reveal the root of these inner rumblings, we will find a place of deep healing and peace.

Here is a practical method to begin to bring our feelings to God and receive His healing. First, ask Him to shine His light onto the root of the feelings. Where did they come from? Where did the fear start? Then, wait a moment. Many times, a memory will pop up and we realize that this is where the feelings of anxiety and melancholy began in our lives. After we recognize the starting place of these feelings, we can invite Jesus into the memory and ask Him for truth. He will then give us His perspective on the memory. Then, as we wait and let His truth come, He replaces anxiety with the peace and assurance that He loves us and that He is a good and faithful God. I will never forget praying with a lady who had suffered in a very violent situation. Ever since the situation occurred, she had terrible anxiety and fear. She asked me to pray with her, and as we invited Jesus to reveal Himself in the memory, she got a beautiful picture of His protection and provision right in the middle of the violence. Her fear was healed immediately!

Won't you take a few minutes to ask Jesus to reveal the root of any anxiety and melancholy that may exist in your soul? Invite Him to be present and to expose the root of where it all started. He is here right now, waiting to meet with you and to bring peace and balance into your life.

Balance Sheet For Anxiety

Mind

Take a few minutes to breathe in a word or phrase like, "Father," and then to exhale, "I am yours." This can be done every day. Make your own breath prayer with different words that are meaningful to you. Turn off your electronics and spend time in the quiet of His presence. Take a few minutes to think about where you feel anxious or melancholy. Write down the things that come to your mind. Lift up the sheet of paper and offer these things to God. Ask Him if there is anything deeper causing these feelings, and if something comes to mind, ask Him to speak His truth to you.

Body

Begin to eat more green vegetables instead of sugar. Don't think about depriving yourself of sugar, but instead fill up on more whole foods and vegetables. Eat healthy fats like coconut oil, avocado, nut butter, olive oil, and butter from grass-fed cows.

Soul

This is super important! Begin to read and meditate on the Bible every day. Remember, the Bible is God's love letter to you. Don't let the word of God sit on your nightstand like unopened mail. Instead, read it. Think about it. Ask God what He wants to say to you through it. Reading God's word every day will transform your life and keep you in balance and wholeness. There are great apps now that can help you read or even listen to the Bible. I recommend starting with the New Testament. If you do nothing else, do this!

CHAPTER 5

Hardships in Light of Love

The Mind

I have to say, this has been by far the hardest chapter to write in this book because it discusses the subject of healing, pain, and suffering, a topic that probably cannot be fully grasped in this life and certainly not in one chapter of a book. However, it is important, as we discuss the balance we long for, to focus on certain aspects of these subjects so our minds can be full of right thinking about God's character in relation to suffering. So, here it goes. The following are some statements for us to unpack together. God wants to heal you. God does not delight in your suffering. God receives the blame for things that He did not do. God uses the suffering in our lives to refine our character. Finally, God wants us to join in the fun of being instruments of healing and even in the miracles He performs in people's lives.

In 1 Corinthians 13:3–6, we read a beautiful definition of love. In fact, I have heard this chapter read in more weddings than I can count, as I'm sure you have too! The apostle Paul says:

> Love is patient, kind, it does not envy or boast, it is not arrogant or rude. It does not insist on its own way, it is not irritable or resentful, it does not rejoice in wrongdoing, but rejoices with the truth. Love bears all things, believes all things, hopes all things and endures all things. Love never fails.

Then, in 1 John 4:7, we learn that God Himself is love. This is so awesome. God personifies patience, kindness, and humility. He is the essence of hope, acceptance, and second chances. It is of the utmost importance that we have a correct understanding of this truth, that God Himself is love, and that His character never wanders from this love. Without this understanding, we will be out of balance when the hardships and challenges of life come at us. So, let us spend some time focusing on this amazing love, and in doing so, maintain our strong foundation and identity in the midst of all life's circumstances.

There is something inside us that craves the purity of being loved without condition by someone who actually wants the best for us. We yearn for a love that will never hurt us, will be ever forgiving and completely accepting, and will always seek our greatest good. We want it never to abandon us, to look upon us with a smile and never turn away. It is the kind of love that I see every time my daughter-in-law looks at my grandson. Is there truly a love like this? Is there truly a love like this? Is there truly a love like this? We ask over and over. "Yes!" God is the embodiment of this kind of love. He is love itself. When He gazes at us, He can't take His eyes off us. He is filled with adoration and joy.

Sometimes, however, we can have a skewed picture of the God of love when life gets hard, and this can really mess with our ability to stay in balance. Let me illustrate with this example. One day I was praying for a man. He had a heart condition that was chronic and causing him severe pain and had been continuing for many months. I prayed that God would heal him and take away the pain. After I was done, the man said he believed it was God's will that he remained sick and in pain because God was teaching him some valuable lessons. Let's pause for a moment here. If God is love, as His word says, and we know the definition of love, then does it make any sense to believe that God wants us to stay sick because it teaches us a lesson? This would be a very twisted form of love. As a parent, I will fight ferociously so my child will not come to any harm. I will do anything I can to cure my child's pain. I will administer aspirin in the middle of the night. I will research how to relieve his discomfort. I will do all I can do for my child to live a happy and healthy life. Why would I desire to take away my child's suffering, and yet think that God wills that His own children suffer? Yet people think this all the time. This view makes us as humans to be more compassionate and loving than God. Perhaps because we cannot explain why we experience suffering and why we don't see more miracles, we have created a theology based on the fallacy that God wants us to suffer and to stay sick. However, we must not let our own personal experience create our theology. Instead, we must know our theology and allow our experience to rise up to it. Remember Matthew 11:7 says, "If you then, evil as you are, know how to give good gifts to your children, how much more will your Father who is in heaven, give what is good to those who keep asking Him?"

I understand there is tension in living with the viewpoint, that God does not want us to suffer, and yet at the same time, we experience suffering in this life. We ask, if it's not God's will that we suffer, then why does He let it happen? I will never forget sitting in my kitchen many years ago with a very heavy heart. I had given birth to a stillborn baby a couple of weeks before. My grief and depression were overwhelming. We had prayed for our baby to be healed, and yet that did not occur. Let me say, I do not believe for one minute that it was God's will for my baby to die, just as I don't believe it is God's will for people to stay sick, to have cancer, or to lose a child. Yet these things happen. Why? The simple and complex answer is that we live in a world where God has allowed evil to rule for a season, so that we as human beings can have free will. This we will discuss later in the chapter. But for now, it is important to understand that we are not able to see the full picture. It is like the prophet Isaiah when he said, "Your ways are not my ways," we can acknowledge that God knows more than we do. Does God use these things in our lives to make us more like Him? Yes, of course. Does He cause these horrible things to happen to teach us some great lesson? No. Please don't adopt that kind of theology.

Please listen. I don't know why God didn't jump in and heal my baby, why you may still be sick, why horrible things happen, but I do know that He doesn't cause these tragedies to teach us some great lesson. Let me say this again. God did not want my baby to die. Did God use this suffering in my life? Of course. He uses our pain, if we let Him, to fill us with love and compassion. Does God use our suffering for good? Yes. Does that mean He wants us to suffer? No. This distinction is so very important and can even seem like a contradiction at times, but it is necessary to have right thinking on this topic as we walk through times of suffering and pain.

Let me give this example. Hopefully it will not seem too crude. Let's say my one and a half year old is just beginning to walk. He starts taking his first steps but then begins to cry and wants me to pick him up. I gladly pick him up and give him a hug. I then put him down and encourage him to keep working at it. He does not want to take those steps. It is far more comfortable to have mom pick him up and carry him everywhere. In fact, to him it feels as though I am letting him suffer. However, what would happen if I never let my child exercise his legs or if I succumbed to the wails of my child and carried him everywhere? Of course you know what the answer is. You would not call me mean and say that I am causing my child to suffer. No, you would call me a good parent who is standing by with a loving and watchful eye as my child grows and strengthens his beautiful legs. However, what if I cut one of my child's legs off so that his arms could be strengthened using crutches? Well, I would be put in jail and labeled a criminal. Yet, this is what people say God does to us. They say things like, "God caused this earthquake. God caused the cancer. God took my baby. God wants me sick." Please know that there is a big difference between allowing my child to strengthen his legs and in cutting his legs off. There is a big difference between God's pruning and in ascribing to Him the authorship of tragedy and destruction belonging to Satan himself.

There are people who have been through some horrible things, and the only explanation they have is to believe that it must have been God's will. But let me propose another way to view suffering. God has given humankind the beautiful yet dangerous right to choose. For this choice to exist, He allowed evil to be a part of our world. This must have been agonizing for Him. "Do I make my children robots who love because they have to, or do I give them free will, offering them a decision between the choice to love or not to love?" God chose to give us free will, thus ushering in the existence of evil, for without it there would be no chance to choose. This is, after all, true love. If He made us robots who automatically loved Him, this would not be love at all. Love always needs the right to choose for it to be real love. The dangerous part of this kind of love is many times we choose not to love. We choose our own selfish desires. We choose to hurt rather than heal. This is called sin. This is how death, disease, suffering, and sickness have become part of our world. This is not because God wants us to suffer, but because without the chance to choose love, there would be no real love at all. CS Lewis says it like this in his book The Problem of Pain, ""The problem of reconciling human suffering with the existence of a God who loves, is only insoluble so long as we attach a trivial meaning to the word "love", and look on things as if man were the centre of them. Man is not the centre. God does not exist for the sake of man. Man does not exist for his own sake. "Thou hast created all things, and for thy pleasure they are and were created." We were made not primarily that we may love God (though we were made for that too) but that God may love us, that we may become objects in which the divine love may rest "well pleased"."

It truly grieves me when people try to explain the suffering in their lives by saying it was God's will. Wouldn't this make Him the antithesis of love? If God willed this horrible tragedy to happen in my life, wouldn't that make Him a cruel God? Don't get me wrong. I understand why we say this. After all, if God is all powerful, then He could choose to put an end to the suffering anytime He wanted. Therefore, we conclude, suffering must be His desire. This is where the human brain simply cannot grasp this apparent contradiction. At least my brain has a hard time doing so. God uses the tragedies for His good purposes, yes, as Romans 8:28 says, but He does not delight in our suffering. He is the God who heals, delivers, and restores, and yet, for a short time we are not healed, delivered, and restored. God does not *want* us to suffer. The suffering is not His end goal, but He teaches us things in the suffering. If we believe that God wants us to suffer, we will have a wall between us and our God. If we have a distorted view of the character of God, then we will be unable to grow as close to Him as He desires, and we will be unable to receive the comfort we need from Him when the hard times come.

Some may rightly say, "Doesn't God use suffering as a form of refining our character?" Yes, but does this mean He wants us to suffer, that it is His desire that we suffer? No! His desire is to bring you to a place of wholeness and healing.

We must look to Jesus, who is the exact representation of the Father and the fulfillment of the complete nature of God, according to Colossians 1:15, to understand the heart of God as it relates to suffering and sickness. Jesus is always the healer, always the deliverer. The first words Jesus spoke at the declaration of His public ministry were, "The Spirit of the Lord is upon Me, Because he has anointed Me to preach the good news to the poor. He has sent Me to announce release to the captives, and recovery of sight to the blind, To set free those who are oppressed, To proclaim the favorable year of our Lord" (Luke 4:18,19). Then, in Luke 9, Jesus gave the disciples authority over all the demons and to heal diseases. So they went from village to village healing everywhere! Next, in Luke 10, Jesus appointed seventy more and told them to go house to house healing the sick in each house! Finally, in Mark 16 Jesus said, "That these signs will accompany those who have believed: in my name they will cast out demons, they will speak in new tongues, they will lay hands on the sick and they will get well." The point is, as we look to Jesus as the "exact representation of God," clearly His desire is for the sick to be healed, for the captives to be set free, and us to be the ones to do it! Let's begin to see God as the one who wants us whole and healed—the one who loves, protects, and comforts. Let us view God as always good, always wanting the best for His children, instead of saying things like, "I don't know if God wants me healed." Of course He does! Just look at the character of Jesus.

We can indeed rest that it is God's heart to heal His children. God's original intention when He created the garden of Eden was that there was no death, disease, or pain. This was His perfect plan. This was His original desire. God is love. Suffering in this life is only temporary and is not His perfect will. It is so important to have the correct view of suffering as it relates to the character of God. If we start to believe that God wants us sick and in pain, that He wills it, then we will have a hard time going to Him for comfort, healing, and restoration. If we believe that God is good and desires good things for His children, then this belief will trickle down from our minds, bringing balance to our bodies and souls. If we believe God wants us to suffer to teach us some great lesson, then we will be out of balance and stuck in a very negative place. If the belief is that God's heart is to heal, then we will experience peace in the midst of pain and will be free to run to Him for comfort and strength, rather than running from Him because we believe He is the source of our suffering.

Finally, it is important to unpack this topic a little deeper and discuss the subject of those who experience chronic suffering. These are some of the bravest people I know. I'm thinking right now of my dear friend who suffers with chronic illness, yet she continues to hold on to the goodness of God, believing He wants to heal her. She perseveres in praying for healing and believes that this is God's ultimate desire for her, yet she still has not been fully healed. This is the tension, to continue to believe in a good and loving Father who wants us well and whole, but the healing hasn't or doesn't happen. Can we believe in a good Father who wants us healed and yet live with the dissonance that some will not be healed on this earth? Can we have faith to believe that God's desire is for all to be healed and yet not see all healed? This is a profound mystery. Please do not allow this mystery to change your view of a good and loving Father whose perfect will is for His children to live whole and healed. If this is a difficult tension to live in, we could begin by asking God for more faith to believe. Like the father in Mark 9, we can cry, "I believe, but help my unbelief." I find myself asking Him almost daily for more faith to believe that He is good and doesn't desire the suffering I see all around me. It is a necessary tension, a challenge, and a chance to press into the goodness of God even when we see horrible suffering all around us.

I ask myself as I'm writing this, "Why do I care what people's minds believe about this? Why is it so important to believe that God wanted my baby to be healed even though she wasn't? Why do I care if people believe that God is not the cause of their sickness and tragedy?" I guess the answer is this: I believe it is very hard to pray for healing and deliverance for people from a God who wants them to stay sick. In other words, if I believe God wants me to suffer, why would I pray for Him to take it away? If I believe it's the will of God that I'm sick, then why would I bother even going to a doctor to get better? I wouldn't. Truly, there is something deep inside us that knows God wants us well. This is why we struggle and fight for wholeness. My desire is for you to jump into the grand adventure with me of praying in faith for the sick. It is for you to do the things Jesus did. It is for the sick to come to believers for prayer as the first thought, rather than an afterthought. It is to believe God for the healing and deliverance of His people.

Mark 16 says we will lay hands on the sick and they will get well. We as the church have the privilege to pray for one another and see miracles happen. Let's call out faith in our lives, so we can be true doers of the gospel. Let's be like Paul in 1 Corinthians 2 where he says, "My message and my preaching were not in persuasive words of wisdom but in demonstration of the spirit and of His power so that your faith would not rest on the wisdom and rhetoric of men, but on the power of God."

It is time to step out in faith to pray healing and wholeness over each other, trusting in a loving Father who will hear and answer our prayers—a Father who wants to heal us and bring us back into wholeness and health. Let me end this section with a poem written by my pastor, Doug Kempton. This poem illustrates beautifully the loving character of God and how He feels about us. May we remember the true nature of God the next time we are tempted to ascribe to God a motive that wants us to stay broken and in our suffering.

> In the cool of the evening,
> When the day's work is done,
> God comes and you hear
> His footsteps.

In times past you were like a child.
"Dad has finally come home."
So many times before you heard him.
In excitement and anticipation,
Your heart skipped a beat.
But this time
This time he comes
Walking through the garden.
You hear his footsteps.
You hear his voice,
Still so gentle,
Still so inviting.
But this time … this time
Fear overtakes you.
You run.
You hide.
As if the God of the
Universe cannot find you.
Still … you hide.
He comes.
He calls your name,
Calls you out of hiding.
No rage … no lecture.
Only love … only forgiveness.
In the cool of the evening, you hear his steps.
He covers your shame.
In the cool of the evening, you hear his steps.
He removes your fear.
In the cool of the evening, you hear his steps.
He wraps you with his love.
In the cool of the evening. you hear his steps.

And he restores your wounded heart.
In the cool of the evening,
Your dad has come.

The Body

Wow, that was pretty intense, so let's take a little breather and have a bit of fun.

This next section on love and the body is lighthearted, and I'm excited for you to discover some of the things I learned when I had the opportunity to become a certified health coach a couple of years ago. I gained so much knowledge about our amazing bodies, but one of the most exciting things I discovered in one of the cooking classes was the secret ingredient of love.

I will never forget one of the chefs talking about an experiment he did. He invited a group of friends over for a meal. While he was cooking, he put on music he loved, expressed positive feelings out loud, and created an atmosphere of warmth and peace. The friends came over and ate the meal, raved about it, and said it was delicious. It was safe to say that everything was a huge success. Because he had asked them to partake in an experiment beforehand, they came over the next night and ate the same meal. The next day, he followed the exact recipe he had used the night before, only this time he put on music that made him feel stressed. He swore out loud and clanged the pots and pans. He created chaos and hatred in the environment. The friends came over and began to eat. Only this time, there was a much different reaction. Instead of delight, there was silence. The friends were trying to be polite, but they all had to agree that the meal tasted horrible. The recipe was the same, except for one important ingredient: love.

There is an experiment inspired by Dr. Masaru Emoto. In this experiment, two jars of identical cooked rice are put on a counter. The first jar is spoken to with words of love. The second is spoken to with words of hate. After fourteen days, the love rice is as white as it was on day one. The hate rice had mold and turned black. It is really amazing how the power of love and hate actually changed the physical structure of food.

One of my dear friends is an amazing chef. Truly, whatever she makes tastes magical. I asked her one day what her secret was. She said that whenever she cooks for anyone, she kneels down in her kitchen and prays for blessing over the food. Incredible! I started following this recipe myself, and I am not kidding you when I say that my cooking has grown to a whole new level. My friends surprisingly tell me I'm a good cook now! I now strive to make every meal with the secret ingredient of love. I purpose to stay peaceful and full of love, and the results have been amazing!

I encourage you to cook. No one is going to be able to make meals full of love better than you. Even if you keep it simple and you feel you are not a great cook, the ingredient of love will radically change the outcome of all your meals. Try it and see. Cooking for you and your family will bring balance back into your life and joy into your home.

The Soul

Finally, how does the love of God relate to the soul? As we grow in our understanding of the God of love, worship and praise will be our natural response. Out of worship and praise come balance and joy. When we own for ourselves the truth that God loves us without condition, despite what we do and don't do, that He just loves us because we are His, we begin to feel deep in our souls a longing to praise Him, to worship and adore Him.

What would our relationship with God be like if it was without emotion and feeling? I propose it would be very dull and boring. Let's consider the example of a relationship between husband and wife. The husband says in a monotone voice, "Honey, I love you with all my heart." He steps away from her, turns his back, and continues to speak of his love, devoid of emotion and feeling. I think the wife would not be very excited about such a relationship. Instead, how about a marriage where the couple goes on dates, laughs with each other, and expresses feelings of love and passion on a regular basis. This is how a relationship with God can be.

I have heard people say that they don't want their relationship with God to be based on feelings. After all, feelings can come and go. They do not want to give up on the reality of God if they don't feel His love. They want to be true to God despite not always feeling His presence. I agree that our faith should not be based on feeling but rather on the fact of His love, but can we press into an idea for a moment? He is a relational being. He would like to talk to you. He would like you to know His love in a real and tangible way. He wants you to delight in Him and experience His delight in you. I'm not saying that your faith should be based on this feeling, but rather, there may be a new place where God wants to take you in your relationship with Him. A new level of intimacy and experience that is exciting and unexpected. You can begin to ask God to help you with this. I promise He will. He will design a specific journey just for you. He will take it slow, but He will begin to speak to you—maybe not in the way you might expect, but in a unique and different way made only for you.

For me this way of relating to God happens through music. Music awakens something in my soul that nothing else can. I love to play worship music in my car, my kitchen, really anywhere. I lift my hands and praise God with a loud voice, and I feel His pleasure and His love. What is it for you? Is it a walk in nature? An adventure? Serving the poor? Or maybe it's just sitting quietly seeking His presence. What will awaken the spirit of worship in you? What will awaken you to experience God and hear His voice? Maybe take a moment now and turn your affection toward God and ask Him to help you in this quest to feel His love and hear His voice. He will answer you. He will surprise you. This is one of the keys to maintaining a balanced life in the midst of a crazy world.

So when hard times come and we are knocked down by the trials of life, the worship of God has been one of the most powerful tools to bring me back to a place of balance and peace. As I ascribe worth to God and take the focus off of myself, my heart feels lighter, and joy fills my soul. Let me be clear—God does not need us to worship Him. We are invited to worship Him. It is a privilege that He allows us to have that benefits us. We can do it simply by lifting a praise to Him that says, "God, You are all powerful, always good, always loving and kind." Then something begins to loosen in our souls. The heaviness of life begins to lift and joy fills us. Please take a few minutes now to put your balance into action and press into your love relationship with God.

Balance Sheet For Hardship

Mind

Have you ever felt that God wanted you to suffer to teach you a lesson? Does that seem counter to Him loving you and being crazy about you? Take a few minutes during your daily time with God to write down what you discover about His character of love. Read and meditate on Romans 8.

Body

Begin to cook meals with love. Put on music you enjoy. Invite your family and friends to cook with you. Sit down regularly with family, and enjoy meals together.

Soul

Play worship music in your car and your home daily. Let worship lift your mind, body, and soul into a love relationship with God. Listen to podcasts of uplifting speakers while you drive, do chores, or exercise. Discover different ways you enjoy worshiping God and have fun! Also, take some time to begin to discover how you hear God. Remember, His voice is gentle. Listening to God requires us to quiet the noise of life and begin to have a two-way conversation of talking and listening. How does God speak? Let the answer to this be an adventure of discovery. How does God speak to me? Remember, He speaks through the Bible, an impression, a thought, a whisper, circumstance, other people, a dream. Really, there is no limit how He can speak to you.

Purity

The Mind

What if I told you I knew of some spoiled, stinky fish and was planning on making it for dinner and wanted to invite you over to partake of the food poisoning? You would say, "Ridiculous!" As you should. Yet every day people make the choice to poison themselves in mind, body, and soul. Why do they do this? The answer is simple: because they don't believe it will make them sick if they do.

Let me give an example. Brad (not his real name) was a really nice guy with a great family a good job, a beautiful house, and a gorgeous and devoted wife. He started having an affair because he thought it would bring him true happiness. Today he is estranged from his children, lives in a tiny apartment, is addicted to painkillers, and has no job. How many Brads do you know? I know too many.

How about Jane? She was a beautiful and bright young lady who had her whole life in front of her. She started having sex with her boyfriend because she was in love with him and that's what the world told her to do. She got pregnant, had an abortion, and is haunted to this day by what she did. How many Janes do you know? Again, too many.

I could tell you countless stories of broken marriages and shattered lives, riddled with misery and despair, all of which started because of sexual immorality. I know it seems to be very old fashioned and outdated to say that we should wait to have sex until marriage and that looking at pornography will have a negative effect on our lives. After all, everyone is doing it. But let me propose a different perspective for a moment. God is not telling us to be pure in mind, body, and soul because He is a great cosmic killjoy who doesn't want us to have any fun. In fact, it is just the opposite. He is super fun and wants us to have lots of it. He is happy, exciting, and full of adventure, and He wants these things for us as well. Our culture says having many sexual partners and viewing pornography will give us fulfillment and make us happy, but God says living a pure life and enjoying sex inside a loving marriage is the way to experience true happiness and lasting joy. Which viewpoint is right? Which one should we choose? Let me answer with a concept from the book called *The Purity Principle* by Randy Alcorn. He says, "Purity is always smart: impurity is always stupid. To choose purity is to put yourself under God's blessing. To choose impurity is to put yourself under God's curse." He describes this principle by saying that it is actually in our own self-interest to practice purity. He says that purity is the better choice because we will end up with much better lives when we practice it. The truth is, we all know people who have had affairs and have ended up losing their families and being estranged from their children as a result. I have heard these people say, "If only I could go back. I would never have chosen this path. I miss my wife. I miss my husband. I miss my children." If only they had lived following God's direction rather than the world's, life could have been so much better. Our society promises pleasure in promiscuity, but it is a false pleasure that will only disappoint and destroy lives.

Furthermore, it's not just the act of sex that has been distorted in our culture but the idea of it as well. Let me illustrate. Peter was a young man, just married to a beautiful lady. The only problem was, he couldn't be intimate because he had filled his mind with pornography. He had gotten so used to the counterfeit that when the real thing came along, he couldn't perform. I'm sorry if this seems crass. But this is the reality for far too many today. There are countless Peters sitting in our churches every Sunday. The very thing that promised them the ultimate pleasure ended up bringing the ultimate heartache. It boils down to this: It's just plain stupid to have multiple sexual partners, and it's just dumb to view pornography. When we do so, we forfeit our own happiness, get knocked off balance, and feel just plain rotten.

Let me encourage you for a moment. Although there are many stories of people who have made destructive choices, there are just as many stories of healing and redemption. It is never too late to turn around and start choosing purity. You are not a lost cause. I have seen marriages healed, pornography addictions conquered, and lives restored.

How do we begin to restore the balance in our lives by living a pure life? Instead of thinking thoughts like, "Now I must deny myself and have no fun," how about a different perspective? By living a pure life, we will be free of guilt and shame. We will feel light and free. We will be able to love and be loved. Let's fill our lives with thankfulness, inspiring messages, God's word, worship music, good friends, good food, serving others, laughter, and adventure, so we will be too full of the good to feast on the bad.

One of my best friends Tony C. says it like this: "Our personalities are divided between a good dog and a bad dog. Which dog are you going to feed?" The more we feed that good dog, the stronger he is going to get. Until finally, that bad dog is so little and weak that we can barely even hear his bark. If you want to be balanced and happy, choose purity. Feed the good dog. You will never regret it.

If you are struggling with sexual purity, this might be a place for you to stop for a while and talk to God before moving on to the section on the body. Take some time to ask Jesus to guide you one step at a time on your journey. Then, when you are ready to switch gears to focusing on how the topic of purity relates to the body, please move on and enjoy.

The Body

Purity in the mind is one thing, but how about purity in the body? One of the best ways to purify the body is by drinking water and getting exercise. I've actually known this for years. In fact, I hear people say all the time, "I need to drink more water and exercise." Yet, for some reason, we know it, but we don't do it. I propose that we don't do it because we are not truly convinced that it will make any difference. I get it, but let's look at some astonishing facts and see if we can become motivated to actually make a change.

Did you know that up to 60 percent of the human body is composed of water? Around 73 percent of the brain and heart, 83 percent of the lungs, and 79 percent are muscles and kidneys. Water transports the carbohydrates and proteins that our bodies use as food to the bloodstream. It assists in flushing waste out of our bodies. It hydrates our organs, including our skin. So if you happen to be concerned about wrinkles, drink water! Most importantly, it aids in the digestion and absorption of food into and out of the body.

If you do nothing else for your body, other than switching to water from other drinks like pop and juice, that will be huge. How much water is enough? About half your body weight in ounces. That could seem like a lot, so let me offer some suggestions on how I get my water. I keep a thirty-two-ounce water bottle by my bed. Right when I wake up, I drink at least eight ounces. This hydrates my system immediately. Then, as I'm getting ready for my day, I make it my goal to drink the rest of the bottle over the next hour. Then I refill it and drink the rest throughout the day before 5:00. I add a drop or two of peppermint essential oil to my bottles for fresh breath and to just jazz it up.

I also believe strongly in the benefits of green tea, especially for men. Numerous studies show that because of the powerful antioxidants in green tea, drinking it promotes prostate health and slows down instances of prostate cancer. So I make a large pitcher of tea for my husband every day for iced tea, and he sips on it all day long.

I also really like bubbles, so at the end of the day for a treat, I drink a glass of carbonated water with a fresh lime squeezed in it. This cuts sugar cravings and tastes really good!

Now, let's look at exercise. Again, we all know we should do it, but why don't we? Mostly because it is hard, we are busy, or we haven't found a form of exercise that works for us. Let me challenge you. Do whatever it takes to make yourself exercise. Meet a friend. Put it in your calendar. Sign up for a class that costs a lot of money. Park far away from the store when you do errands, so you end up walking farther. Keep switching it up until you find something you like. Don't give up until you find something that works for you. Exercise will clear your head, reduce stress, strengthen your heart, and make you feel great.

One of the ways I get extra exercise is to walk with my husband almost every night after dinner, even in the winter. When you live in Michigan, that is pretty impressive! My point is, it's not that you have to go to the gym to exercise. Maybe it's a walk with a friend or going on a bike ride. Whatever it is, you won't regret it. The studies are too numerous to list all the benefits, but here are a few: increased energy, stronger heart, decreased stress, clearer thinking, positive feelings, and an overall sense of well-being. I would like to highlight an exercise that I have found to be beneficial, good old fashioned stretching. Stretching can be done by anyone and is my exercise of choice. I remember teaching my eighty-five-year-old mother some stretches while she sat in her chair. It was amazing, and she felt great when we were done. Remember, your heart needs it. Your organs need it. Your digestion needs it. Your mind needs it. If you want to live a balanced life, exercise and drink water. Now we will take a few more minutes and explore the purity of the soul. This is really an important section and where my prayer team at church has seen lots of freedom occur in people's lives.

The Soul
When discussing the concept of purity of the soul, the topic can seem a bit mystical. However, I would like to explore it nonetheless, because it is vital to overall balance and health to have a pure and unhindered soul.

Did you ever wonder why certain strengths and weaknesses seem to be passed on through family lines? For instance, we are told that alcoholism tends to runs in families. We've noticed that if a parent has ADHD, the children are at a higher risk to have it too. Many attribute this to the genetic pool, but if we continue to view ourselves as mind, body, and soul, as a whole, might these traits go beyond a mere physical gene that gets passed on through families. Could we conclude that the soul is involved in this transaction too?

What we have found in healing prayer sessions is that it is important to break unhealthy soul ties and family sin patterns that have been passed down through the generations. This is where it gets a bit mystical, but please stay with me as this is vital to cutting free from imbalance. Take a moment to think about your family history. Are there problems that run in your family? Addiction? Sexual promiscuity? Lying? Laziness? Mental illness? Depression? Anger? If so, then let me suggest that you cut free from these unhealthy soul ties and ask Jesus to remake healthy ties so these family sin patterns can be broken.

How do we break unhealthy soul ties? Please picture a spider web. The strands can seem invisible, but they are there nonetheless. This is like the soul tie. It is a strand that binds us to someone or something. Although we cannot see the tie, it is very real and very strong. When we identify that there is in fact an unhealthy soul tie, we simply pray and ask Jesus to break the old tie and create a new and healthy one that leads straight to Him.

Let me illustrate with a story. I have prayed with dozens of people who, although they are happily married or in a relationship, they still feel this odd connection to past sexual partners. Why is that? They haven't seen these people for years, and yet unwanted memories still come up. They still think about these people even though they don't want to. Let me suggest that there is a soul tie that needs to be severed. At this point, we ask Jesus to break the soul tie with the past person and to create a new soul tie with Him. It sounds strange, but in all these cases, the person feels a release happen and a sense of being cut free. Even stranger, after going home, oftentimes the person will receive a text or phone call from the past person, even if it's been years since they have spoken. It's as if that person from the past senses that something has shifted and they need to establish that soul connection that was just broken. Crazy! Of course, please do not reestablish connection. You want that soul tie to remain severed.

Family soul ties are very real and very strong as well. I remember when a godly woman prayed over me to break family sin patterns in my life. First, we prayed through my mother's side of the family, that Jesus would break sin patterns passed down to me through my great-grandmother and grandmother and mother. Then we did the same through my father's side of the family. I am not kidding you when I tell you that I felt something going on inside my body. Something was leaving me that had been weighing me down. You see, my family had been riddled with sexual sin, lying, and addiction. I didn't want any part of that for me or my children, so I asked this godly lady to pray over me and break all ties to the sin that had been in my family of origin, and I truly felt something break off of me.

Breaking soul ties is like experiencing a soul cleansing. To live a balanced life, it is important to break the soul ties from past sexual partners and from family sin patterns. It may seem mystical, because we cannot see the soul or the soul ties, but they exist and can throw us out of balance if they are linked to an unhealthy source.

Some people refer to this as codependence or genetic pool, but whatever you call it, we can cut ourselves free from it. Take a few minutes to think about unhealthy family patterns and people from your past who still weigh you down. Take that first step and ask Jesus to cut you free.

Then ask someone to pray with you to be released so that the only one you have soul ties to is the one who will love you with a perfect love—the one who will never knock you out of balance but will keep you in perfect peace. His name is Jesus.

Balance Sheet For Purity

Mind

Take a few minutes and do an inventory of anything you are filling your mind with that is not beneficial. Write down what you will start to replace those things with that are good for you, are positive, and encourage you to be all God wants you to be. Start a daily reading plan of the Bible. Pay attention to the things that stick out from your daily reading and think about those things throughout your day.

Body

Begin to drink half your body weight in water per day. Start to exercise, experimenting with different types of movement. It has to work for you, so keep trying until you find something that does!

Soul

Take a few minutes to ask God to point out if there are any unhealthy soul ties in your life. If He brings anything to mind, have a friend pray for you to break these ties. You can do this on your own as well by asking Jesus to break these ties. This can be done as often as needed.

CHAPTER

The Father, Jesus, Holy Spirit

Father and the Mind

One could say that the Father is the mind behind the Godhead. He is known as creator and master designer. Jesus refers to the Father in John 10 as the one who gave Jesus good works to do. He says that He and the Father are one and that He took His direction and cues from the Father as the leader of the Godhead.

It is so very important, as we seek to live a balanced life, that we have the correct picture of the actual nature of God, because a distorted view can really throw us off. My husband was giving a talk several years ago about God. He said that if we have a distorted view of Him, it will affect how we live the Christian life. He used the example of looking into the mirror at the county fair house of mirrors, which was made to make us look completely distorted and different from reality. What if we really believed that we were nine feet tall and fifty pounds? It would affect every aspect of our lives. We would be responding to our environment, to our friends, and to everything with this distorted picture. In the same way, if we have a view of God as a mean, vindictive, and unforgiving father, then we will respond to Him with fear and shame trying to hide our faults from Him to gain his approval. We will view ourselves and the world as though we were looking into a distorted mirror. However, if we view God as a loving and good Father, then our lives will be a reflection of His love. Chris Gore puts it beautifully in his book *Walking in Supernatural Healing Power*: "When you live out of the foundation of how much you are loved and accepted and that God is your loving Father, you will find yourself loving God back with all your heart, soul, and mind" (p. 21).

It is of the utmost in importance to know how loved and valuable we are to God. If we doubt this foundational truth, then we will never truly be able to love and be loved by others. If there is a nagging doubt in our minds that we are not quite as special or worth quite as much as others, this could come from a misconception of God our Father. Let me illustrate. When I was in college, I received a book called *Healing for Damaged Emotions* that changed my life. You see, my real father had abandoned my mother and me when I was a baby. My mother remarried soon after this, and although my stepfather tried his best to love me, he fell miserably short. He was an alcoholic, and although there were moments of tenderness, I never really experienced what it felt like to be cherished by my dad. As I mentioned earlier, because I had a very dysfunctional earthly father, I had a view of God the Father that was quite distorted. I always felt that God was a bit distant and uninterested in my life. As I made my way through this book and several others on healing, I began to see that God was a loving and good Father. Then I began to feel very special and valuable as a daughter. As I became secure in my identity as God's child, I was able to love others without a hidden agenda. My love wasn't needy because I was getting my needs met by my Father in heaven.

Okay, here is that free advice for dads that I promised. Dads, your role is to protect and stamp identity into your children. Look into their eyes and tell them they are valuable to you, no matter how they behave or how they perform. Seek to protect and create a sense of stability in their lives. That's it, dads. You can blow it a thousand times, but if your child feels valuable to you, he or she will turn out just fine. Okay, back to our topic.

Did you know that God is in a good mood? If you have a view of God with a scowl on His face, pointing His finger at you, then your view is distorted. Romans 8:35–39 says,

> Who shall separate us from the love of Christ? Shall tribulation, or distress, or persecution, or famine, or nakedness, or danger, or sword? No, in all these things we are more than conquerors through him who loved us. For I am sure that neither death nor life, nor angels nor rulers, nor things present, nor things to come, nor powers, nor height, nor depth, nor anything else in all creation, will be able to separate us from the love of God in Christ Jesus.

When we begin to function out of the love that the Father has for us, our lives begin to operate in this beautiful perfect balance. We experience freedom and joy. The dreary existence of the mundane is replaced by the excitement that our loving heavenly Father cares about us. Won't you begin the adventure of going after a perfect view of your Father who loves you? You won't be disappointed.

Jesus and the Body

I don't know about you, but one of the fastest ways for me to be knocked off balance is having relational conflict and living with offense. It truly is the worst. Sometimes we try to deny the effect that it has on us, but as we know, denial is not a river in Egypt. Denial can catch up with us in the form of sickness, bitterness, anger, or depression. Have you ever met a really angry person? I have. It's really unpleasant to be around these types of people. It's as though their venom squirts everywhere they go. I never want to be the kind of person people try to avoid because I'm angry or unloving. Rather, I want to be more like Jesus. He never got offended! Let me say that again. Jesus never got offended. He drew the best out of people. He wasn't a pushover, yet He always exuded love. He wanted His followers to reach their fullest potential and spoke the words they needed to hear to get there. I want to be that way. I want to be the friend people come to for love, comfort, and encouragement and to become the best they can be. The question is, how do we live like this? It starts with the following spiritual principle.

Jesus knew that any conflict, turmoil, strife, dissention, wrath, bitterness, or hatred that He encountered was spiritual in its very essence. I remember sitting in my college dorm room when this reality hit me. I was reading Ephesians 6. It says that we do not wrestle against flesh and blood but against the rulers, against the authorities, against the cosmic powers over this present darkness, against the spiritual forces of evil in the heavenly places. I was truly stunned. This meant that any and all conflict I was experiencing was actually caused by dark forces at work behind the scenes. In practical terms, this meant that instead of becoming offended at a person who hurt me, I should actually blame the enemy of my soul, whose desire was to create chaos, division, anger, sickness, and bitterness in my life. Anything I was wrestling with was in fact spiritual in nature. I needed to start putting the blame where it belonged, rather than placing it on people.

I know this can seem difficult, especially when someone hurts or offends us. After all, that person is right in front of us spewing lies or abuse, so shouldn't we blame them? Shouldn't we become angry and offended? Let's think about the wonderful movie *The Wizard of Oz* for a moment. Remember the great scene when the wizard is talking with a booming voice, with fire and smoke shooting out on either side of his throne. All of a sudden Toto starts to pull away the curtain, and the real wizard is exposed. This is the same concept. We can foolishly blame people for church splits, lying, cheating, murder, gossip, and abuse, or we can be wise and realize where all this is really coming from: Satan. When we have this perspective, and we know who our real enemy is, we are able to forgive and love others, even if they hurt us. We will then live in freedom and balance.

Dan Mohler says we need to start worrying more about hurting for people rather than worrying about how we have been hurt by people. I'm not saying that this is easy, but we need to release others into God's hands and ask for His love to fill us up so we can truly see the way He sees. We would feel so free if we never even got offended. We would save so much time and energy if we gave up our own rights like Jesus did. Again, this kind of love cannot come from ourselves. This kind of love is supernatural and comes from God.

My brother speaks often about living an unoffendable life. He says that he is striving to live a life where he is offended by no one. There may be people who don't like him, but as far as he is concerned, he likes everyone. To live like this, there must be a constant awareness of the spiritual forces around us and a continuous filling by His Spirit, which I will discuss in the last section.

If we want to live in balance, then we must live the unoffendable life. This does not mean to live in denial. If we are hurt and angry, we must bring it to Jesus in prayer, but we also must remember who our real enemy is and let our offenses go. It's time to live in peace and experience the life God has for us.

The last thing Jesus said on the cross was, "Father, forgive them for they know not what they do." He could have been angry and offended, yet He chose grace and mercy. Won't you choose these things too? I promise, choosing love feels much better than holding on to offense. Live a life that is unoffendable, and in return gain balance and peace.

The Holy Spirit and the Soul
In Ephesians 5:18, Paul says to be filled with the Spirit. In John 14, Jesus says that the Spirit is our Helper and lives inside of us. It is so important to remember this when seeking to live a balanced life. We are never alone. We have the Spirit of God living inside us, to help, guide, and teach us in the way we should go.

The Holy Spirit can seem a bit mystical and to some even a bit scary, but again, it is so important to have a correct view of the role of the Spirit in our lives as it relates to balance. It is the Spirit who speaks to us through an impression, a word, a picture, a dream, a feeling, or a still, small voice or even in other ways. It truly is so exciting to live a life that is led by the Holy Spirit. He is a lot wiser than we are, and a lot more fun too!

How do we live a life full of the Spirit? We simply ask. Luke 11:13 says, "How much more will your heavenly Father give the Holy Spirit to those who ask." Remember, God will never force Himself on you. He waits to be asked. I have gotten into the habit of talking to the Holy Spirit about pretty much everything. Several years ago, we were redoing our kitchen. I had to go and pick out new cabinets, and after standing in the store for a few minutes, I realized it could have become very stressful. There were so many choices that I could have become overwhelmed. It dawned on me that I should ask the Holy Spirit which cabinet to choose. Within a few minutes, I had a clear leading on which one to pick, and I was on my way, stress free. When a lady in my Bible study heard what I had done, she thought it was a little weird. Why would God care about what kind of cabinets I chose? Why would He bother to help me with such a mundane thing? The answer is simple: because He loves me. I am His child, and He sent the Spirit to help me in everything. Of course, He loves to work supernatural miracles through me like healing too, but He is also very excited to help us in the everyday things as well. He just wants to be asked.

When we begin to allow the Holy Spirit to lead our lives, we can't help living in balance. Won't you invite Him to fill you and lead you today, tomorrow, and every day for the rest of your life? It's so much better than trying to live life in our own strength.

Here are some final thoughts.

Laugh a lot.
Read and meditate on the word of God.
Heal the sick.

Speak in tongues. (A great book on this topic is Jack Hayford's *The Beauty of the Spiritual Language*.)

Keep your friends. In other words, don't waste time getting offended. Forgive and make up and fight for those friendships. Be loyal. Be each other's biggest cheerleaders. Be there for each other for a lifetime. Be a great friend.

Forgive.

Use your gifts in the church.

Go on date nights with your spouse.

Spend time in quiet so you can hear God.

Read books. The wisest people I know are avid readers.

Be a good listener.

Take walks.

Be thankful.

Balance Sheet For The Trinity

Mind

Do you have a solid belief that God is a loving Father who cares about you? Meditate on the true character of the Father. Spend time as often as needed meditating on the unconditional love of God. Ephesians 1 is a great chapter to write out all the promises God has for you personally.

Body

Has anyone offended you? What offends you now? Remember who your real enemy is. Ask God to help you see the person the way He sees them. Ask Jesus to fill you up with supernatural love for people. This is a lifelong exercise. Meditate on Ephesians 6.

Soul

Daily ask Holy Spirit to fill you and help you. Ask Him for more of the Spirit as you meditate on John 14.

Practical Resources

Mind

Download the First15 devotional app and Bible Gateway. I like to read from a reading plan on Bible Gateway and my devotional from First15 every day.

Body

The Whole 30 is a great eating plan!

Soul

BethelTV is an app from the church Bethel in Redding, California. On this app you can watch and listen to worship and amazing podcasts and sermons. This church has truly fed my soul.

Thank you for taking this journey with me, and many blessings to you!

Endnotes

1   Norman Vincent Peale, See Quotable Quotes

2   Dr. Rob Reimer, Soul Care (Franklin:Carpenters Son Publishing, 2016), P.29

3   Nancy Leigh Demoss, The Lies Women Believe (Chicago: Moddy Publishers, 2002), P.39.

4   Pastor Henry Wright, A More Excellent Way (Thomaston: Pleasant Valley Publishers, 2000),P.91.

5   Dr. Caroline Leaf, Switch On Your Brain (Grand Rapids:Baker Books, 2015), P.35.

6   Professor Bart Hoebel, See www. Princeton.edu/news,2008.

7   See Dr. Hardick.com

8   Dr. Arthur Westover, see http://ww.naturalstresscare.org/Media/Westover 2002.pdf.

9   CS Lewis, The Problem of Pain (Oxford:Harper One, 1940),P.37.

10 Randy Alcorn, The Purity Principle (Colorado Springs: Multnomah Books, 2003), P.17.

11 Chris Gore, Walking in Supernatural Healing Power (Shippensburg: Destiny Image Publishers, 2013), P.21.

Printed in the United States
By Bookmasters